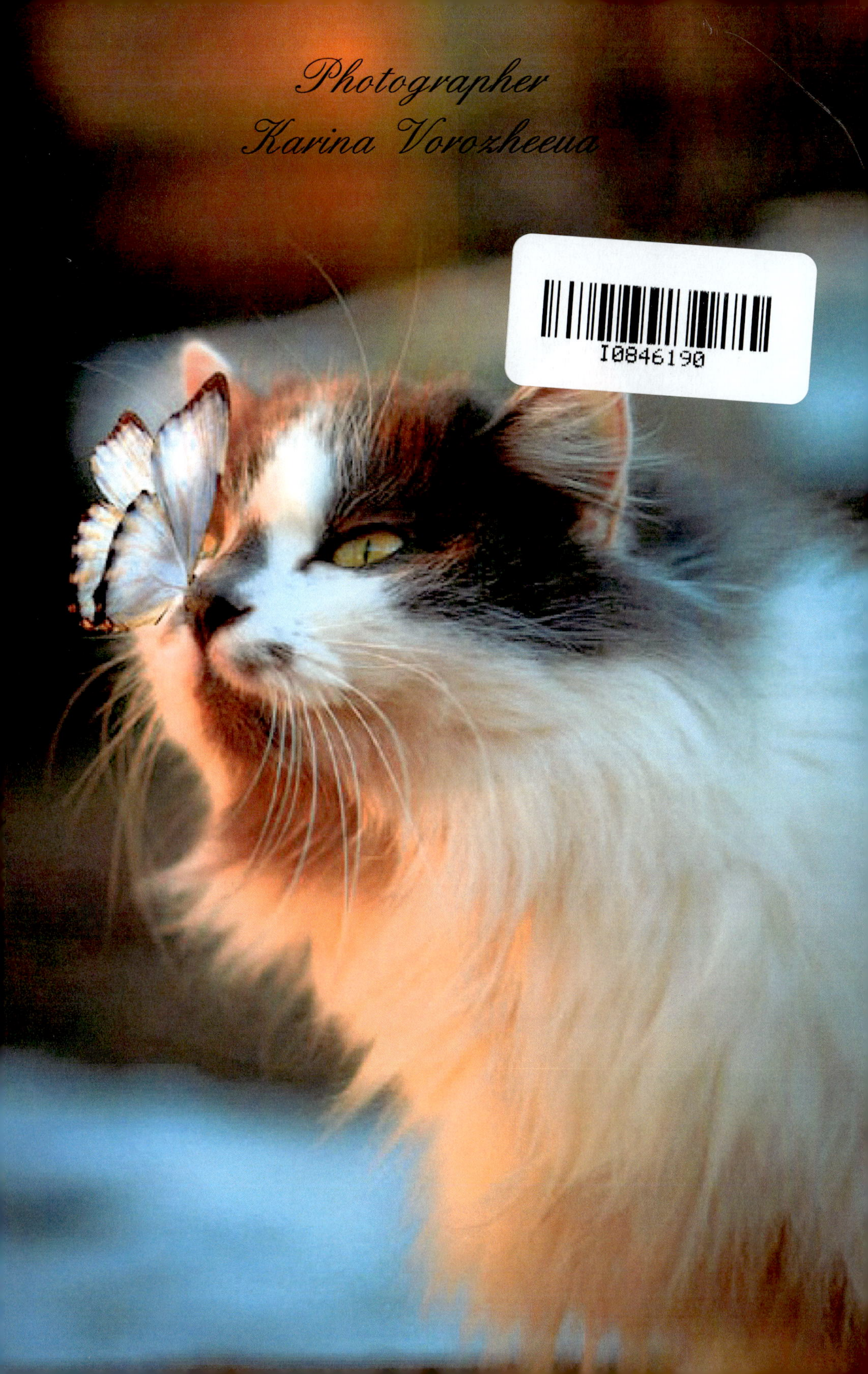
Photographer
Karina Vorozheeua

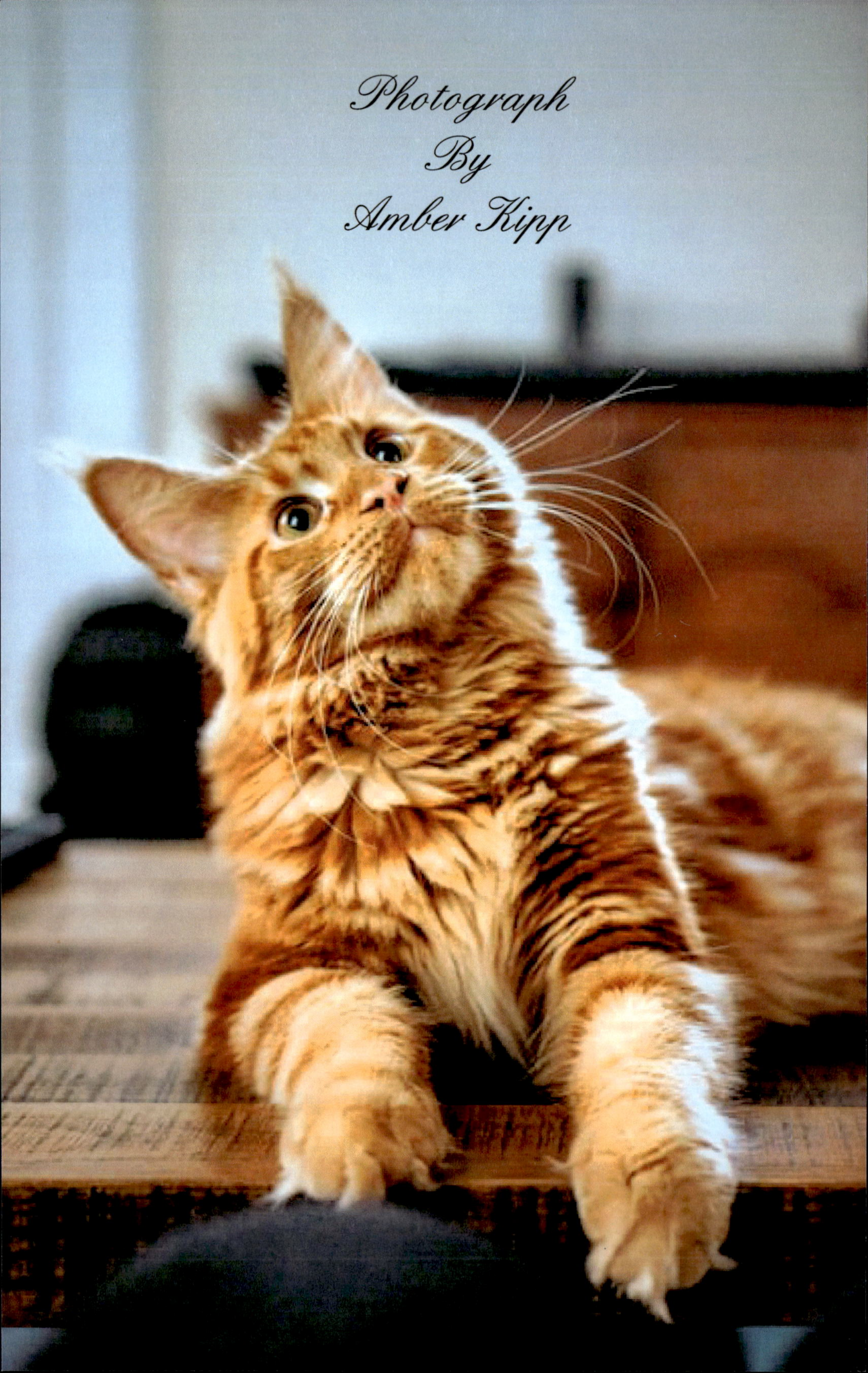

Photograph
By
Amber Kipp

Photographer
Aline De Nadai

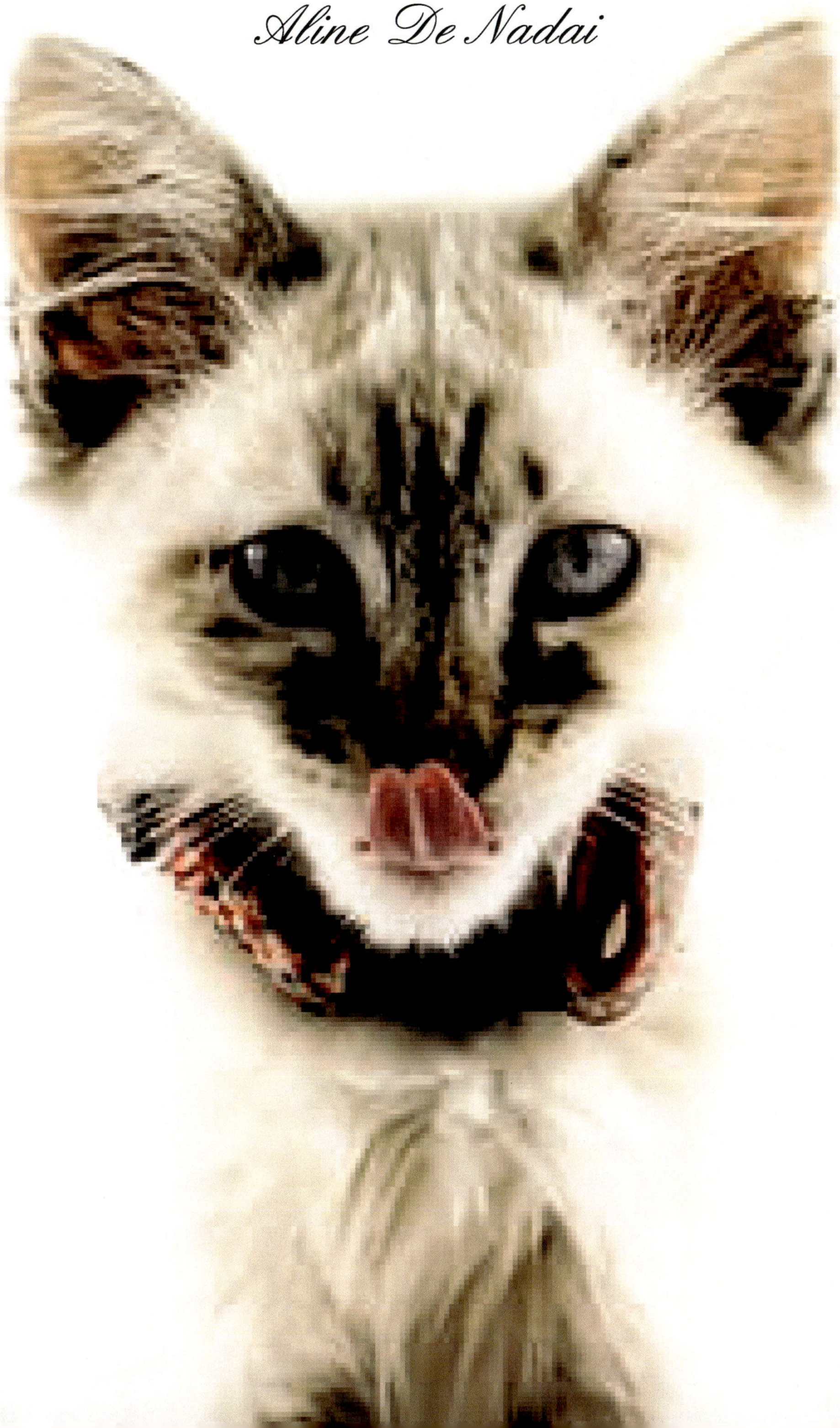

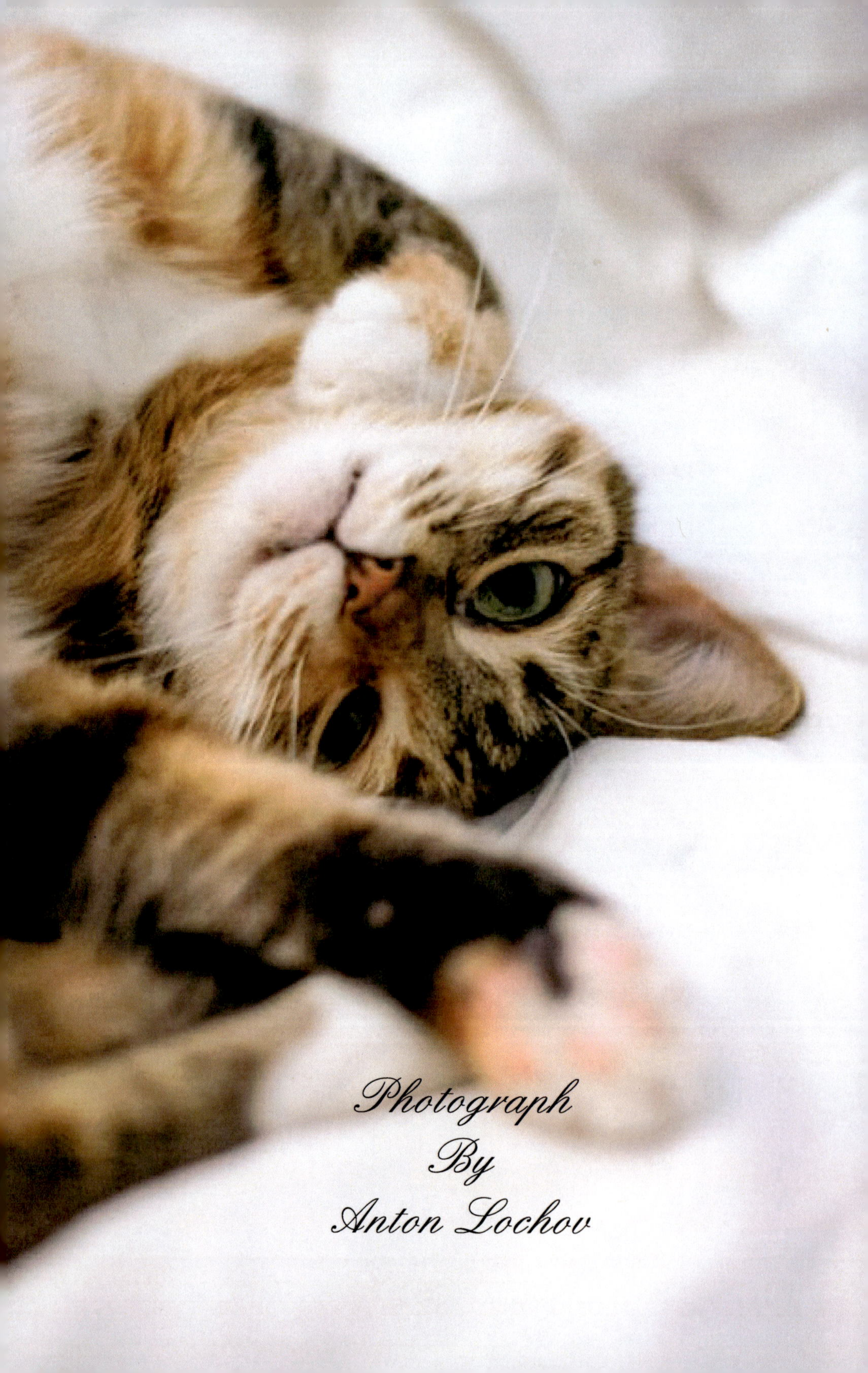

Photograph
By
Anton Lochov

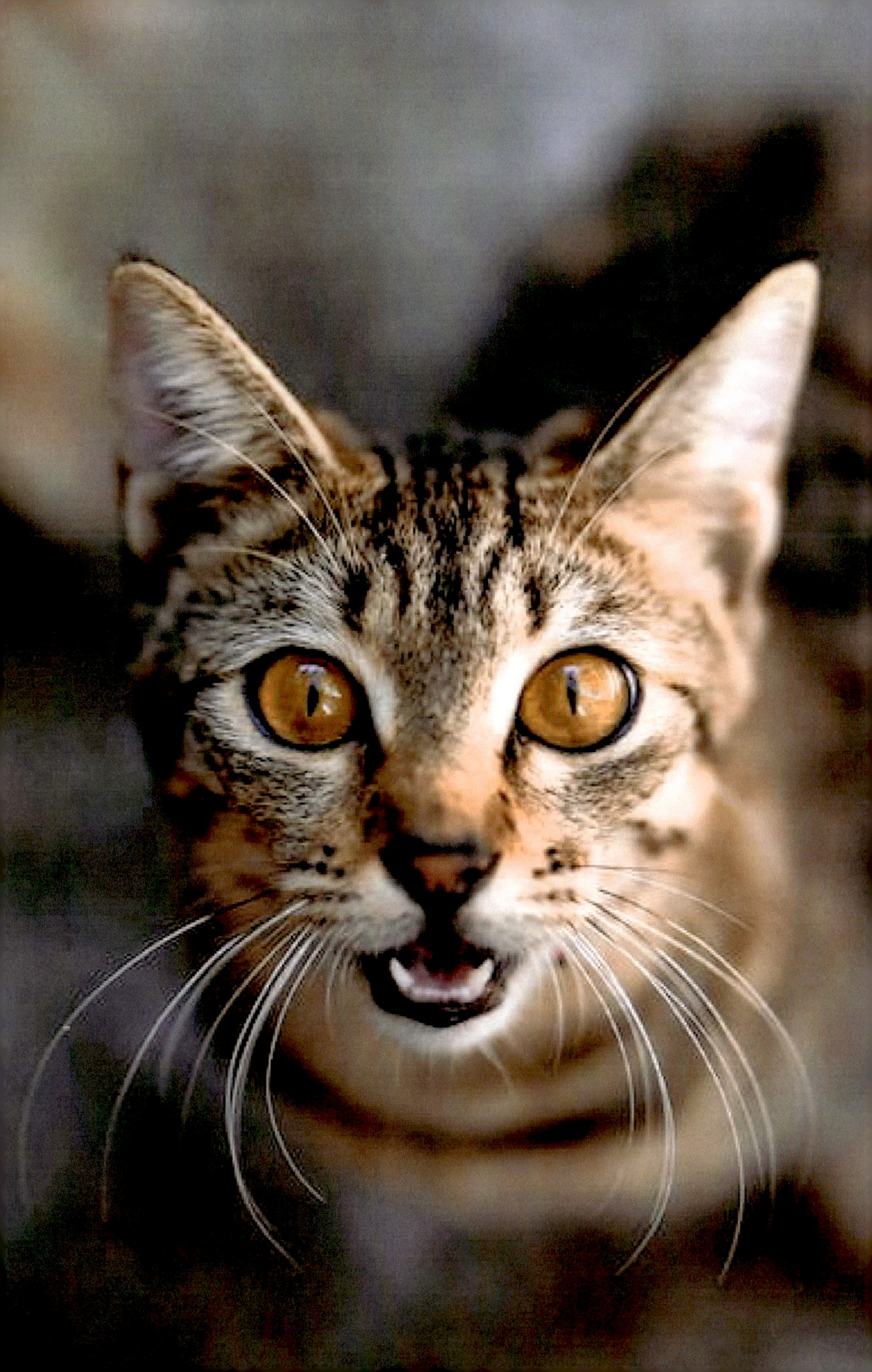

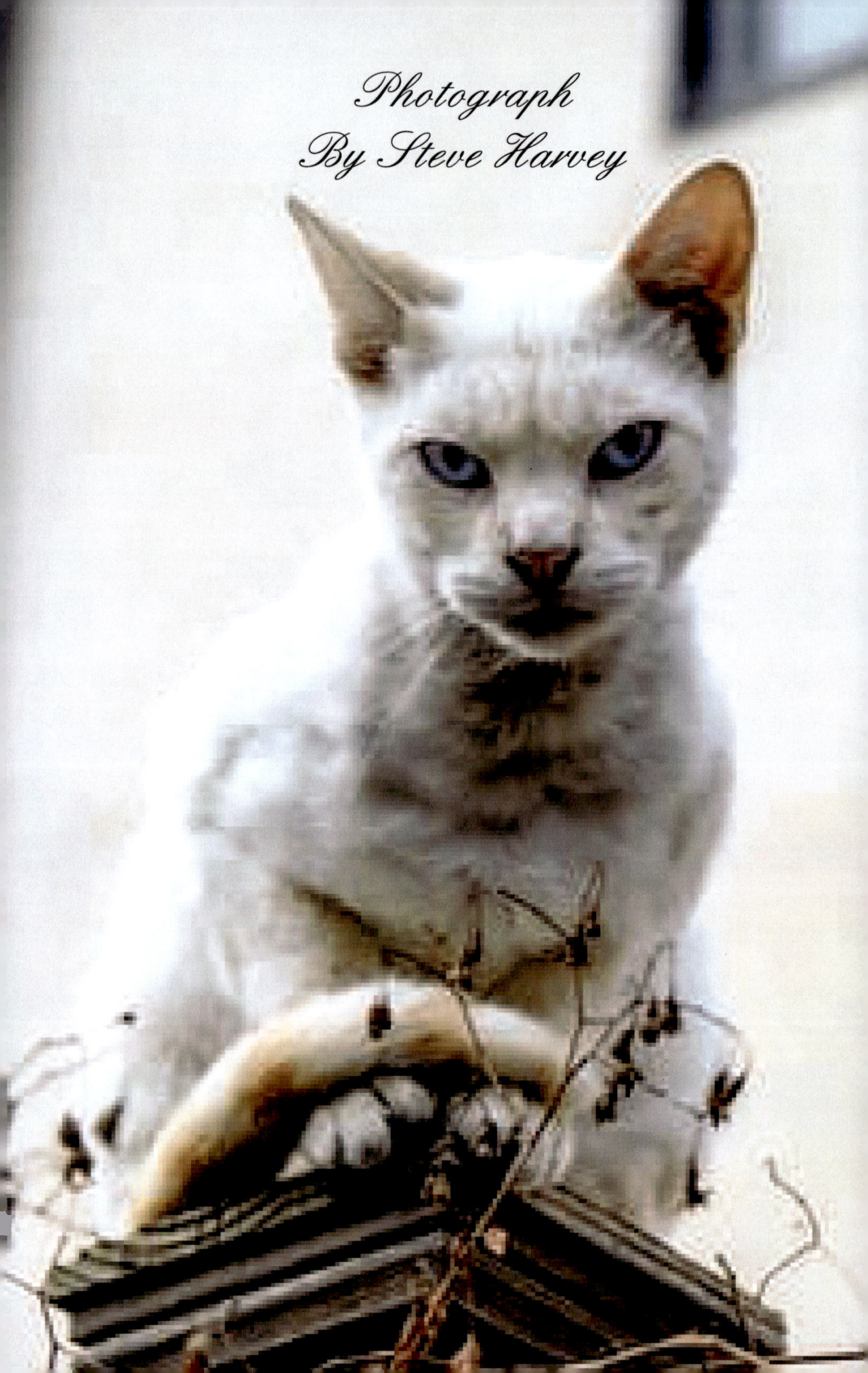

Photograph
By Steve Harvey

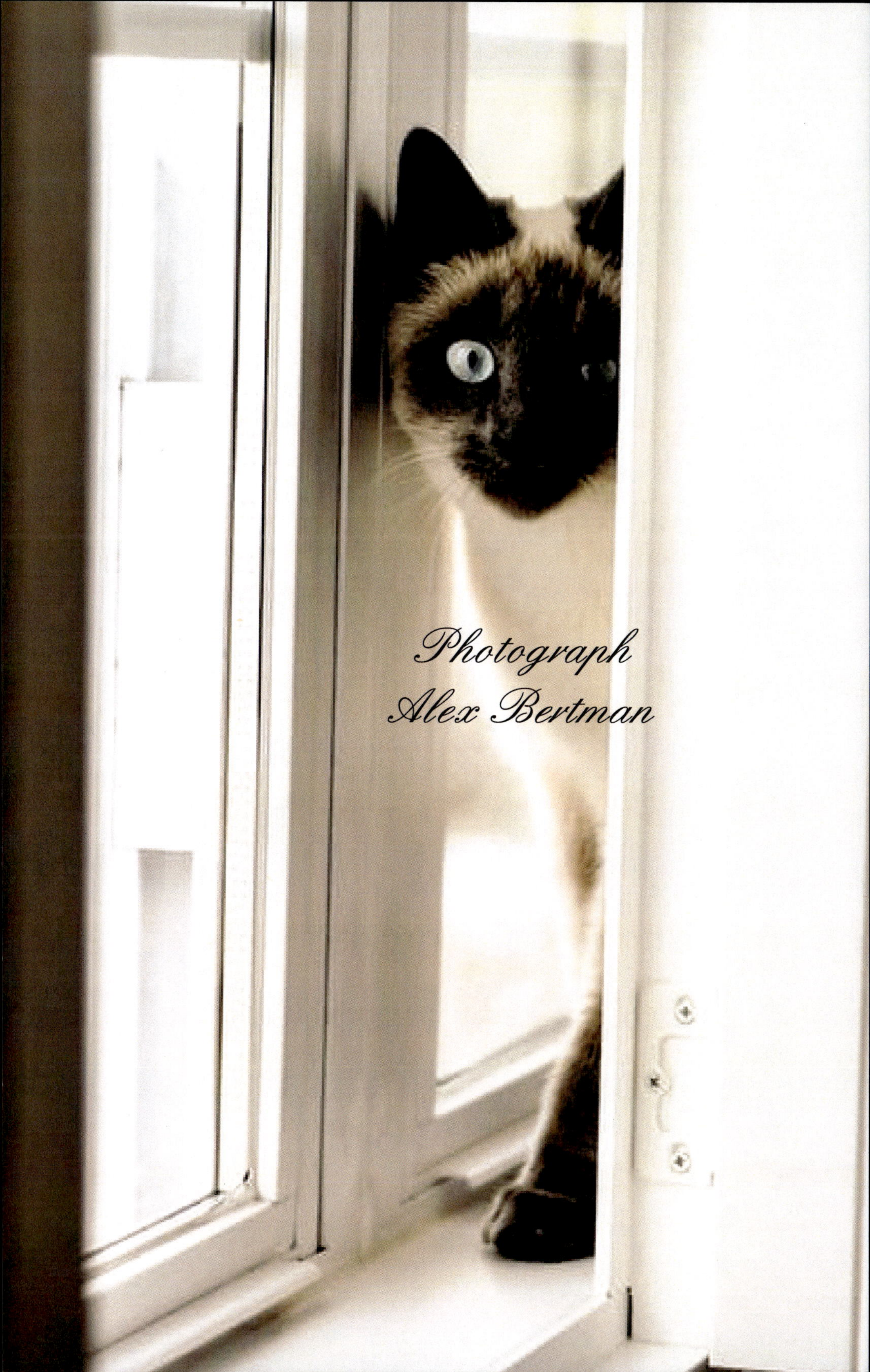
Photograph
Alex Bertman

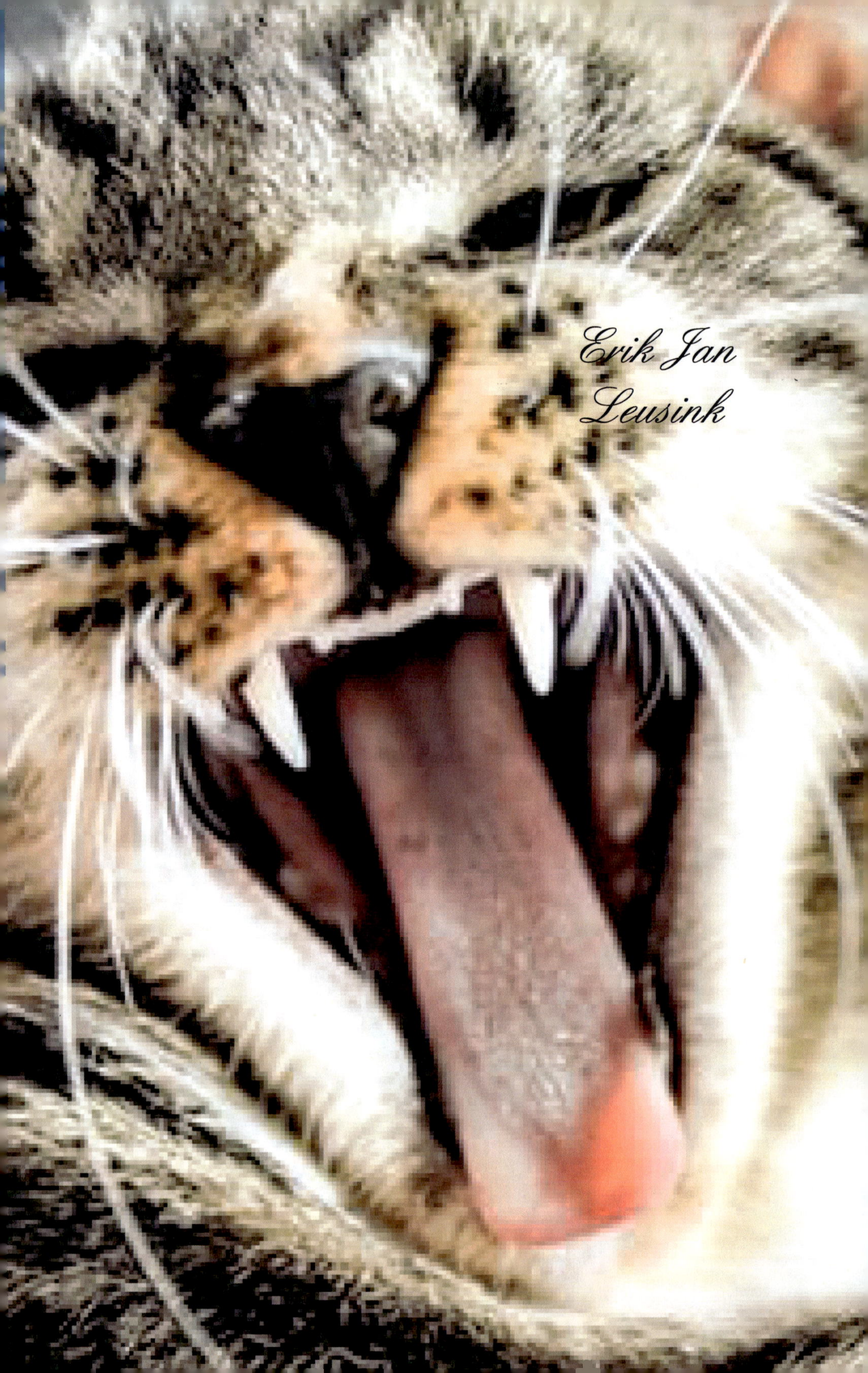
Erik Jan
Leusink

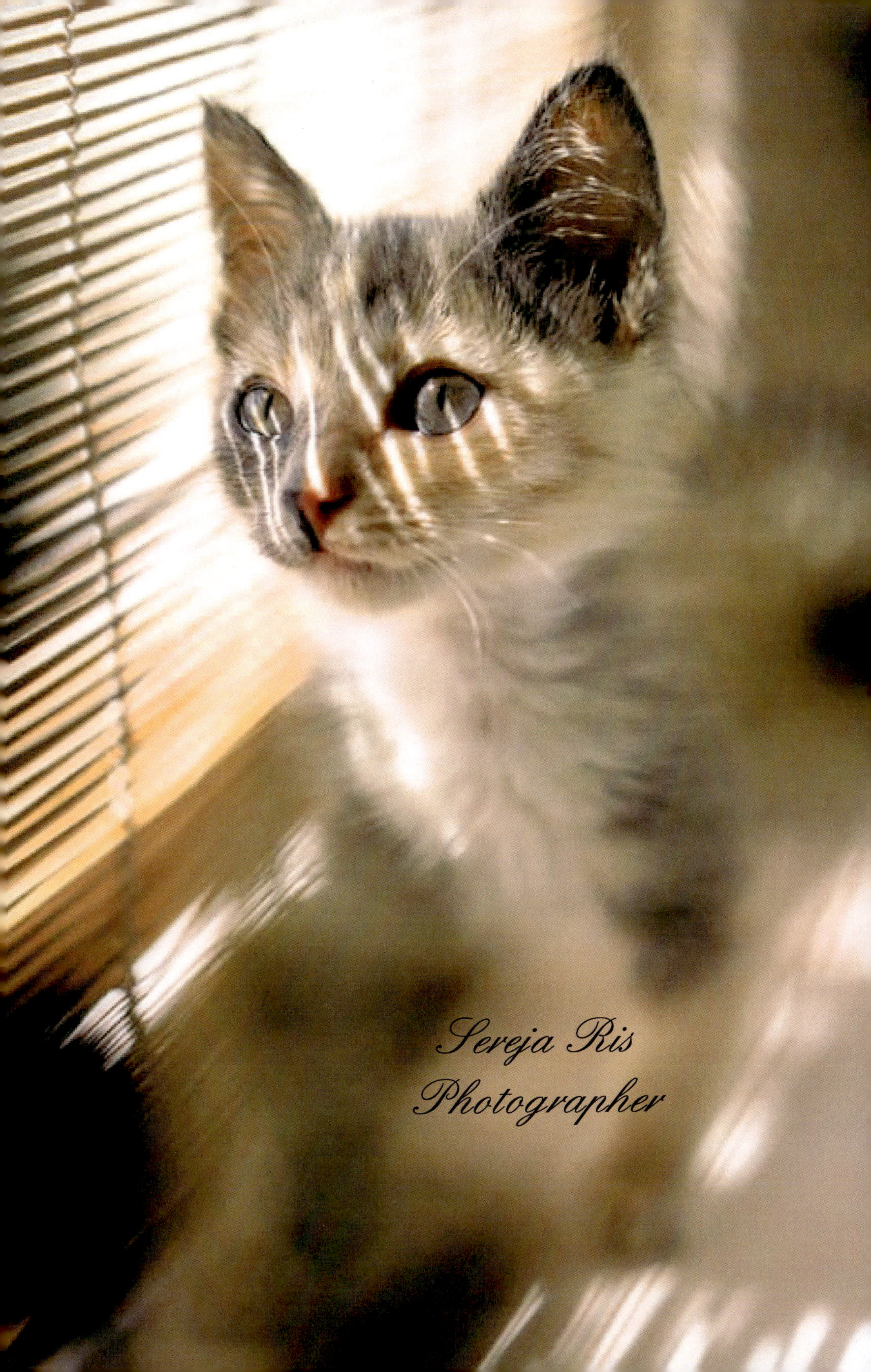
Sereja Ris
Photographer

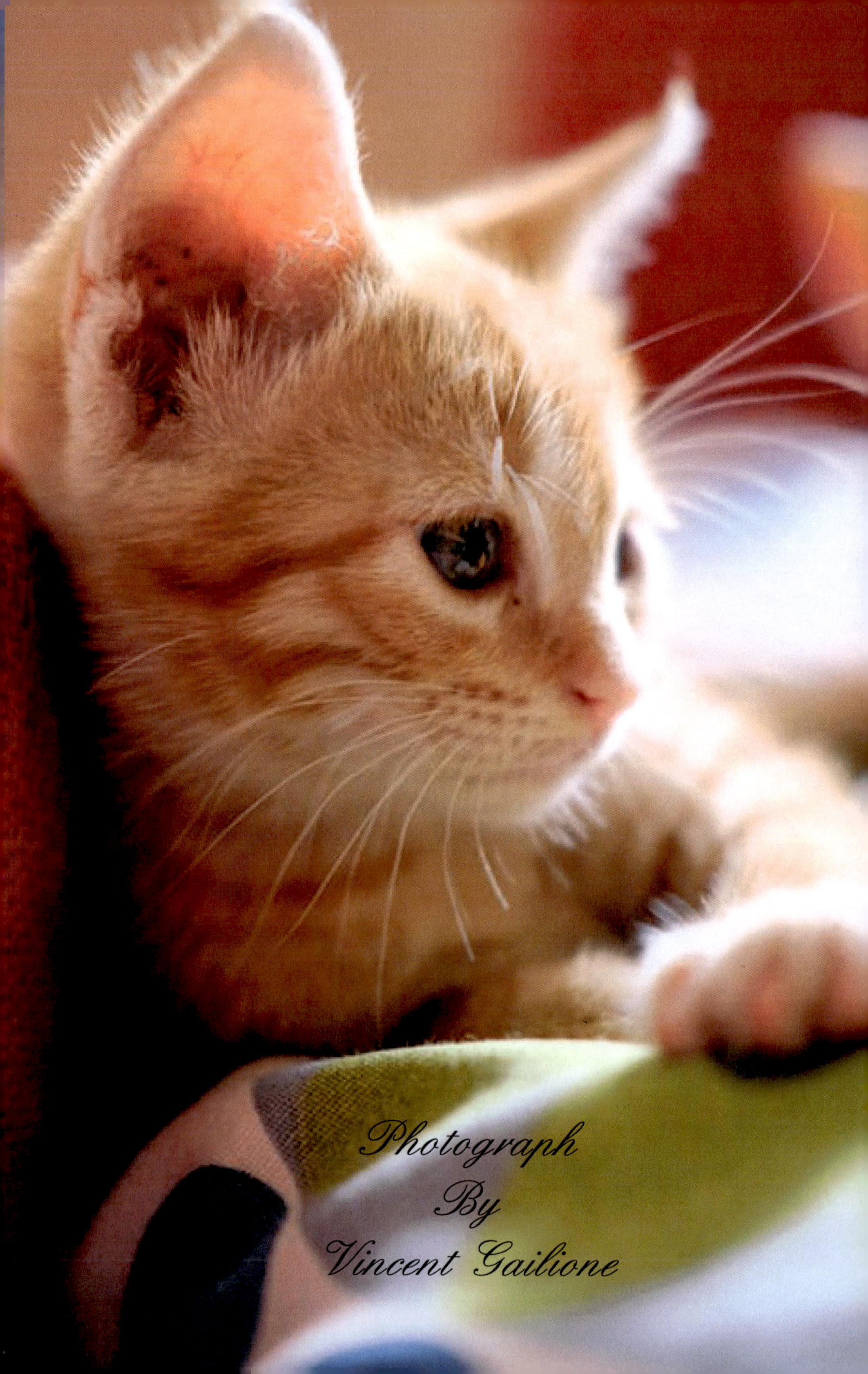
Photograph
By
Vincent Gailione

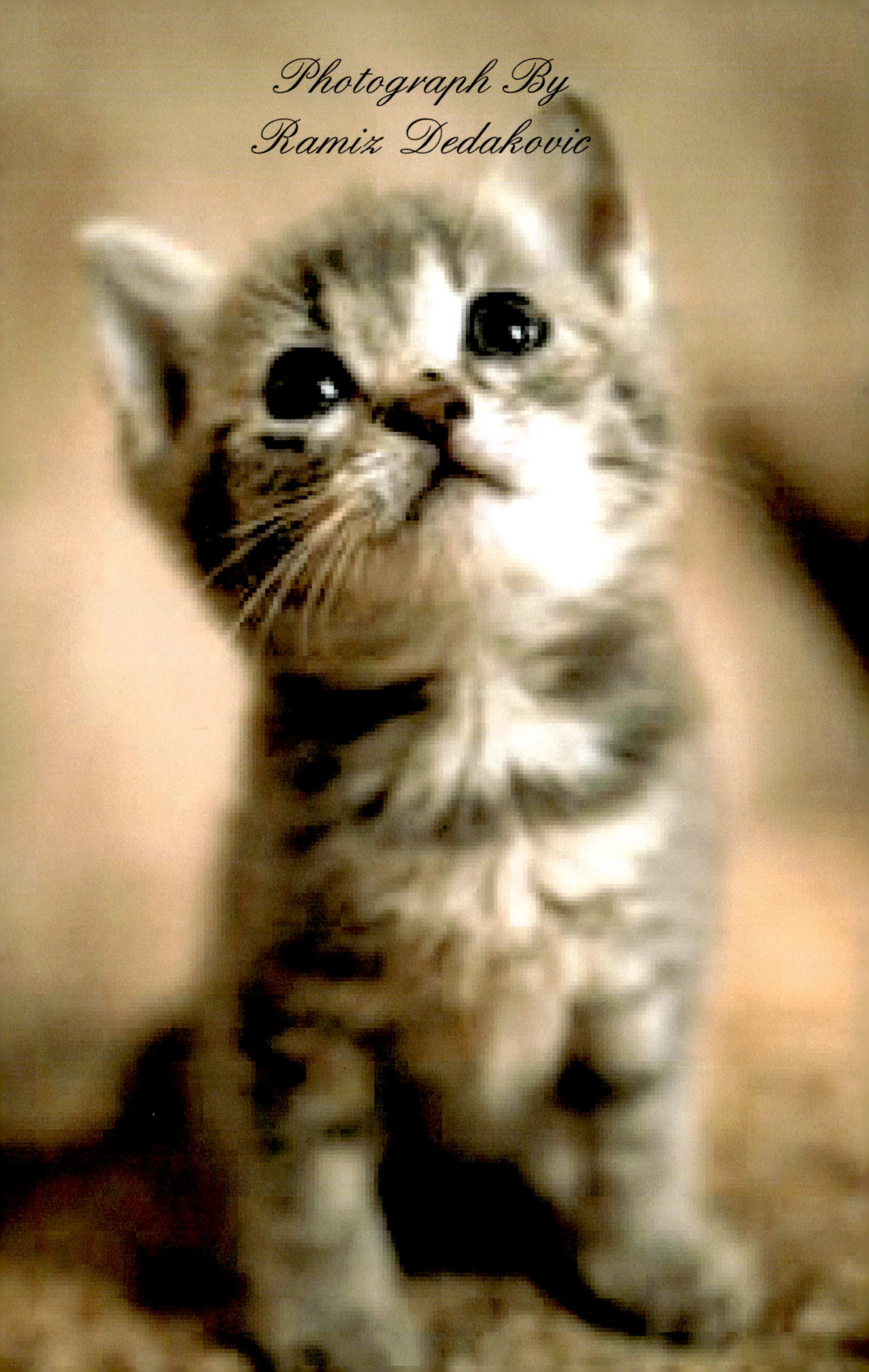
Photograph By
Ramiz Dedakovic

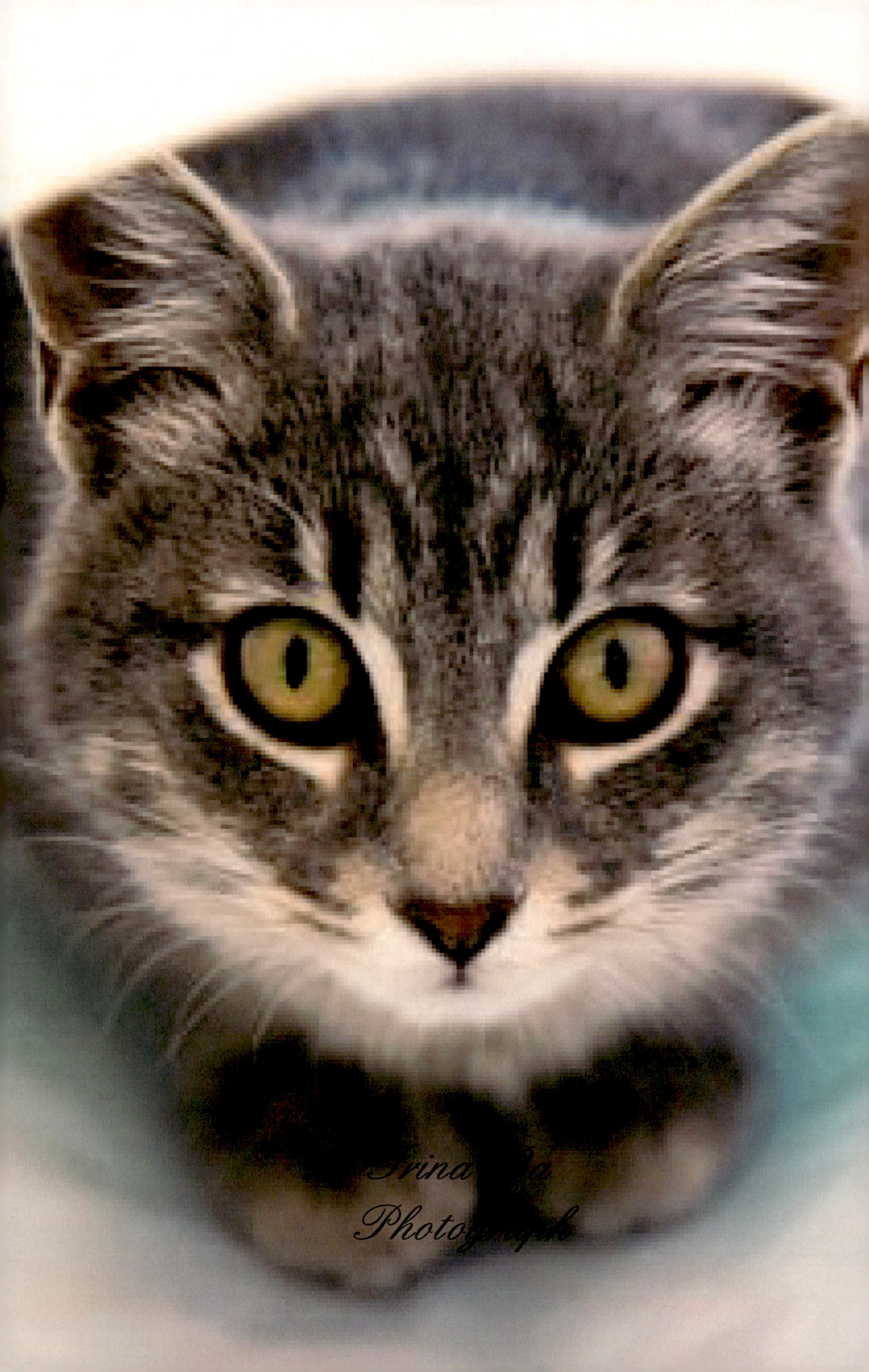
Irina

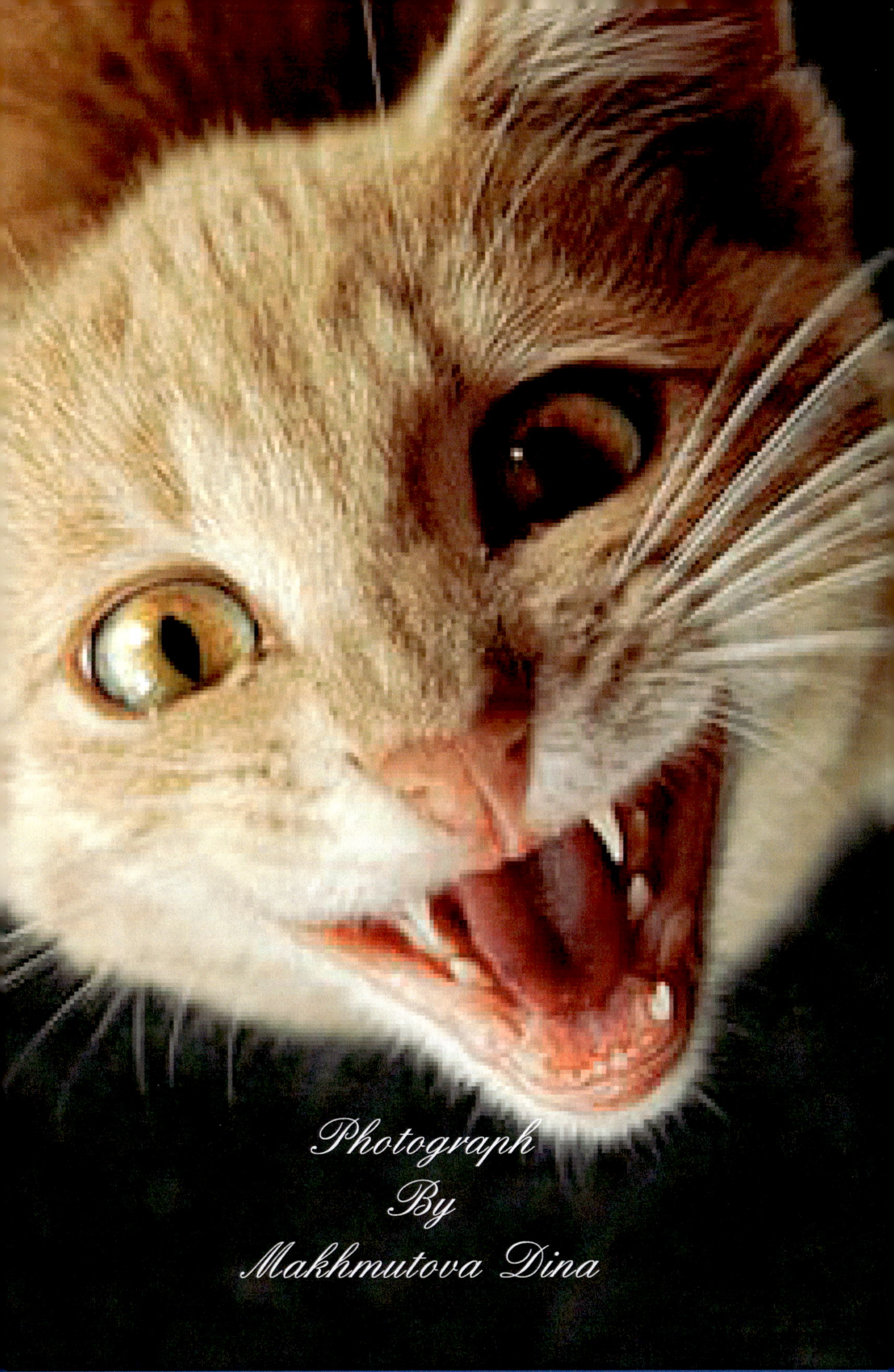

Photograph
By
Makhmutova Dina

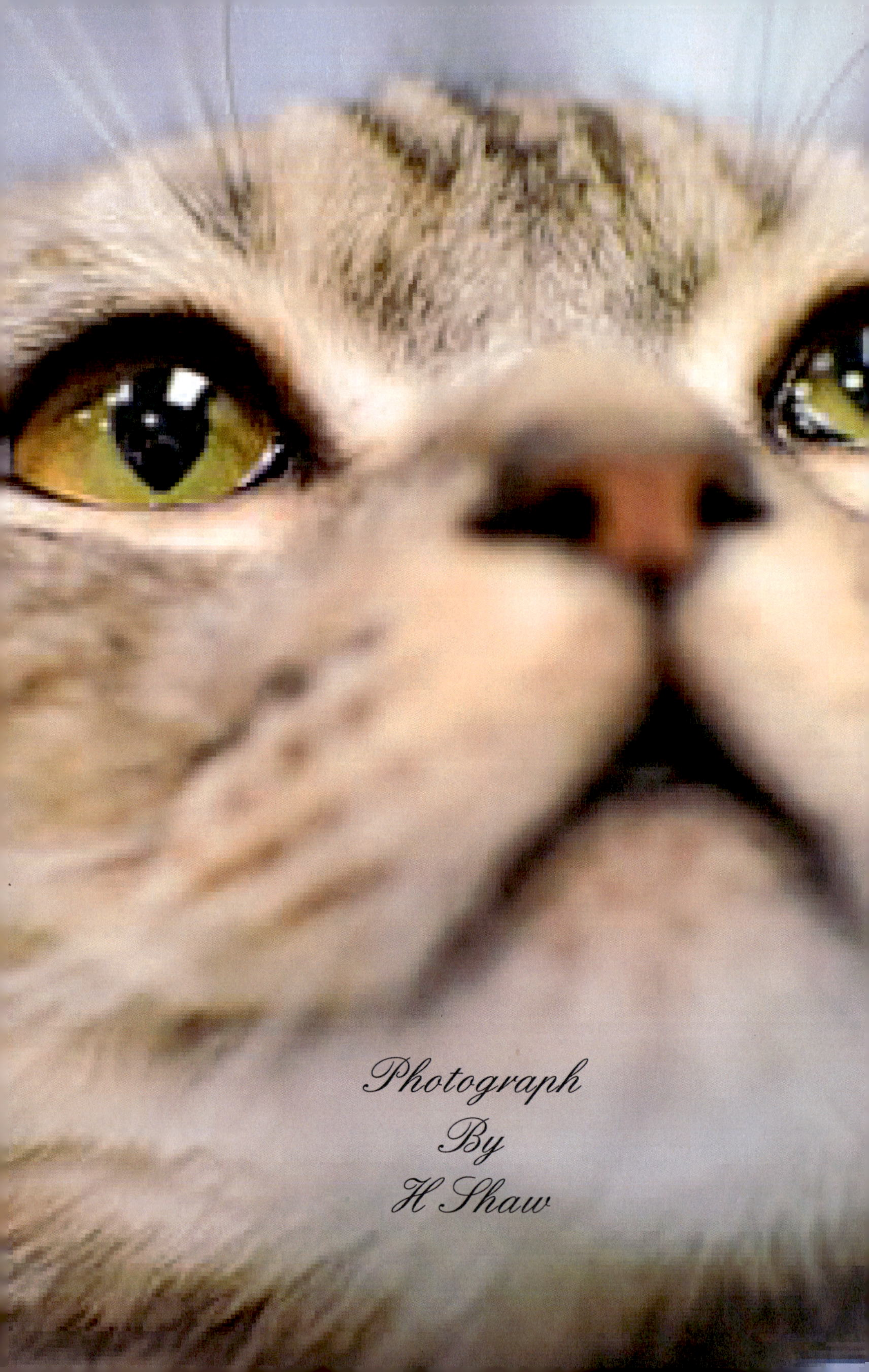

Photograph
By
H Shaw

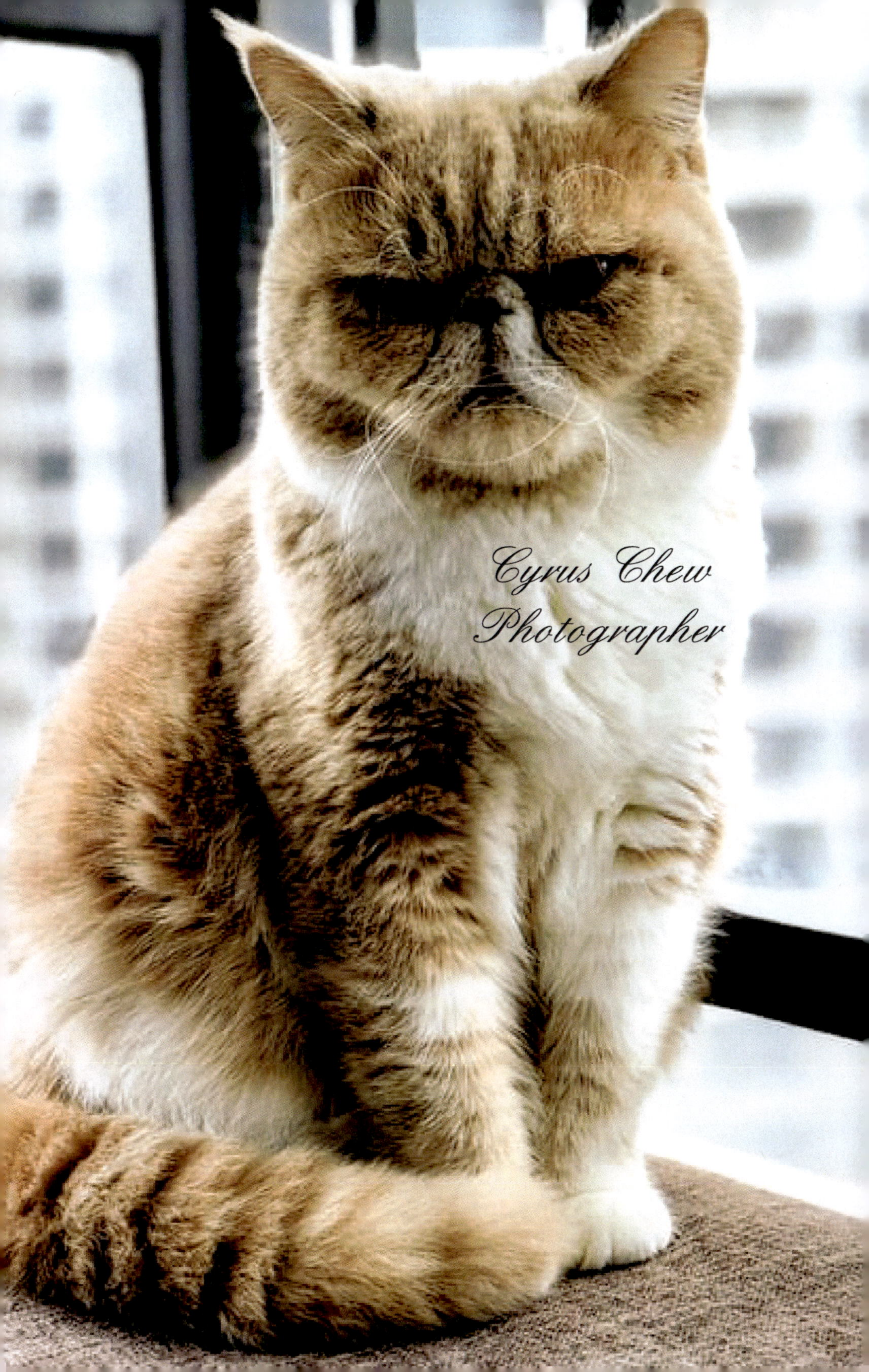
Cyrus Chew
Photographer

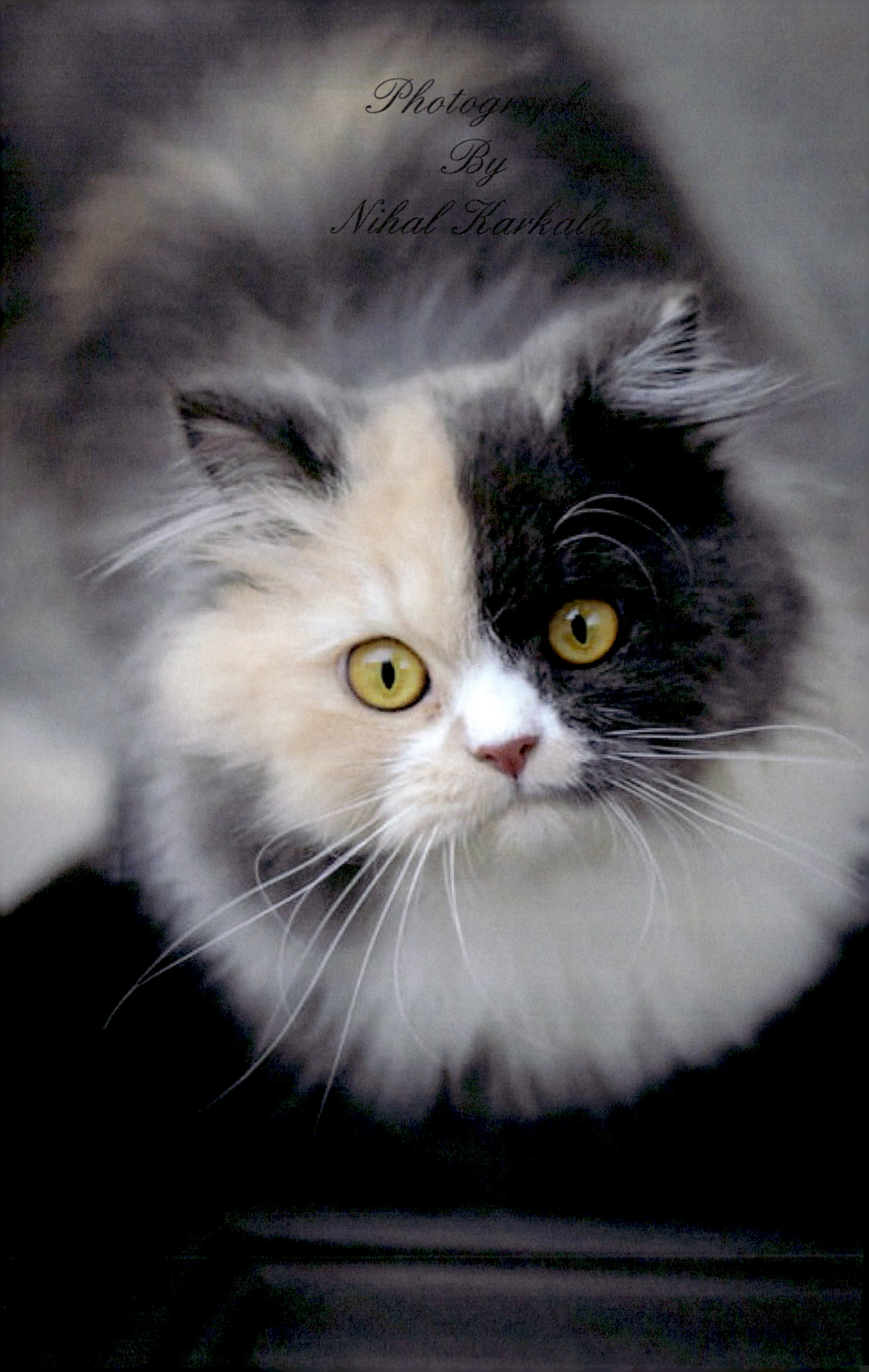
Photog
By
Nihal Karkal

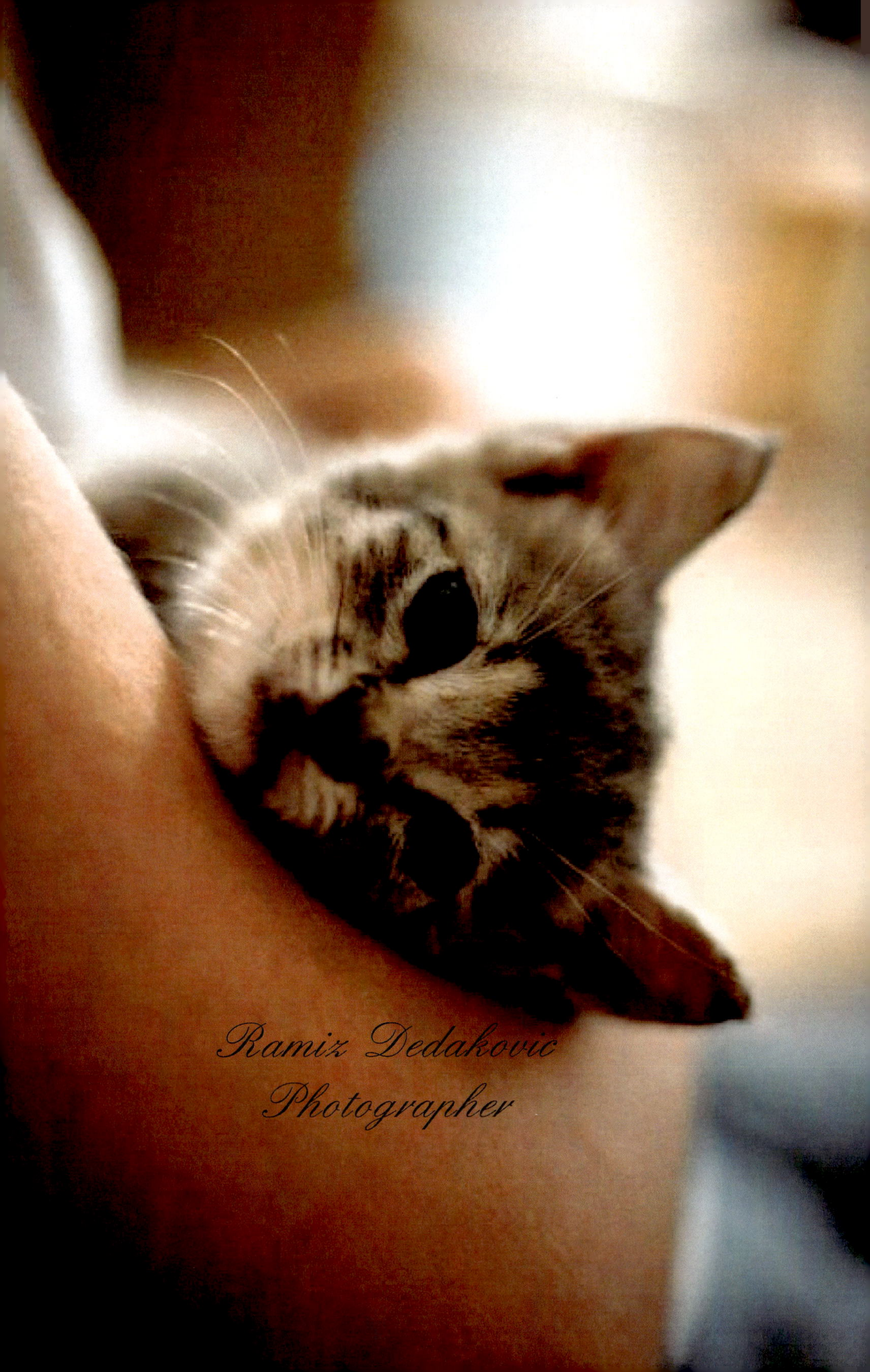
Ramiz Dedakovic
Photographer

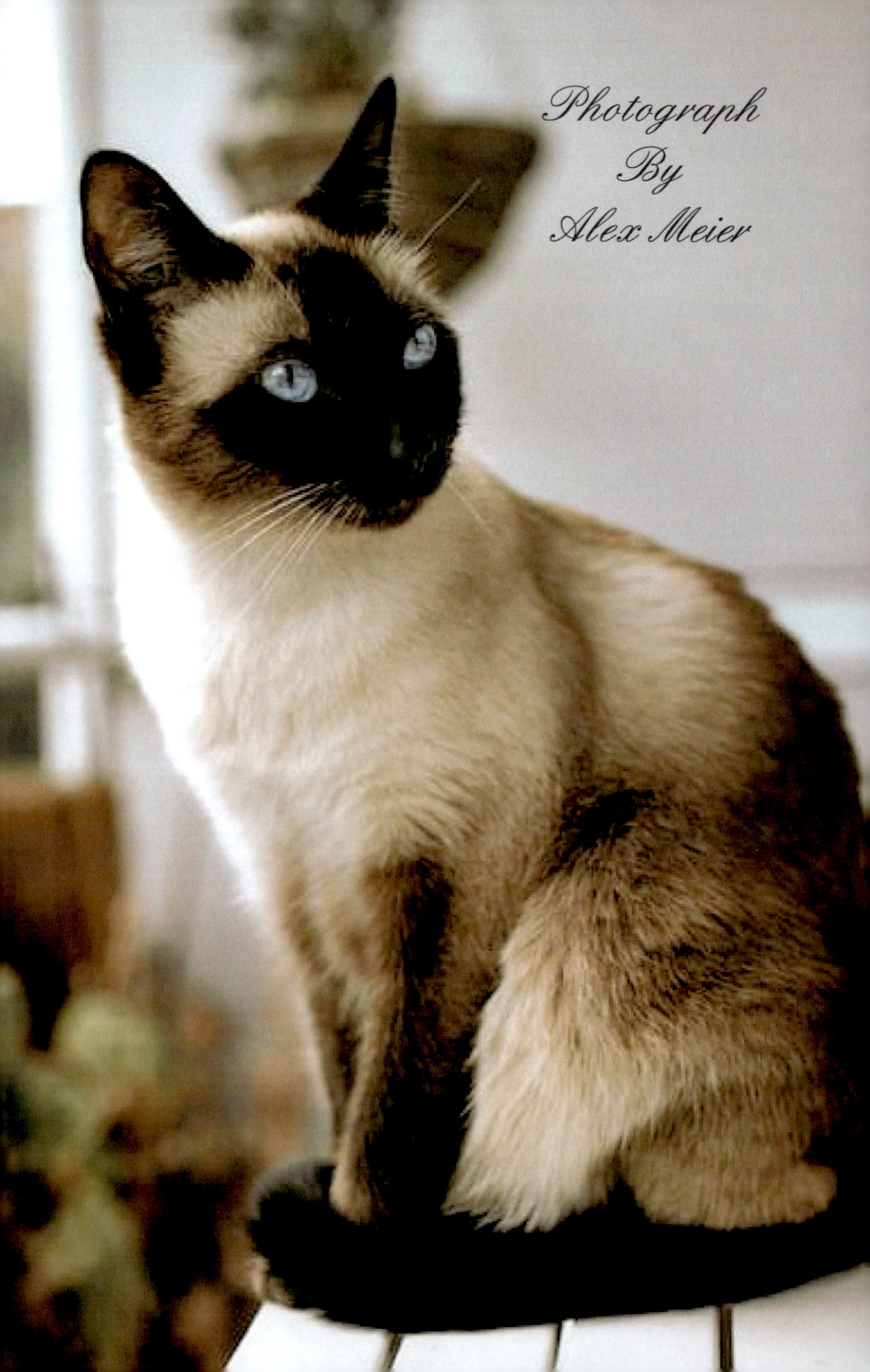
Photograph
By
Alex Meier

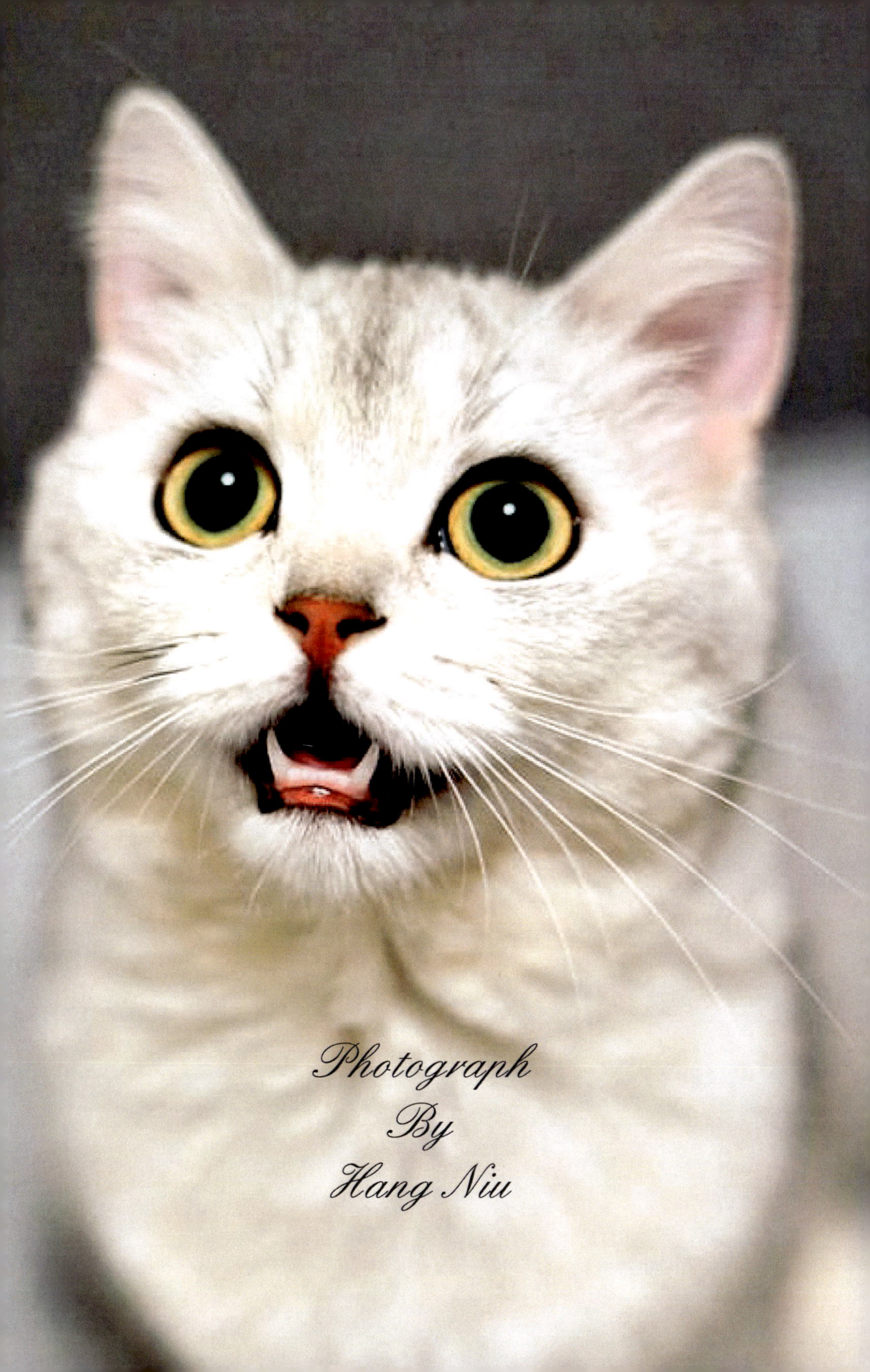
Photograph
By
Hang Niu

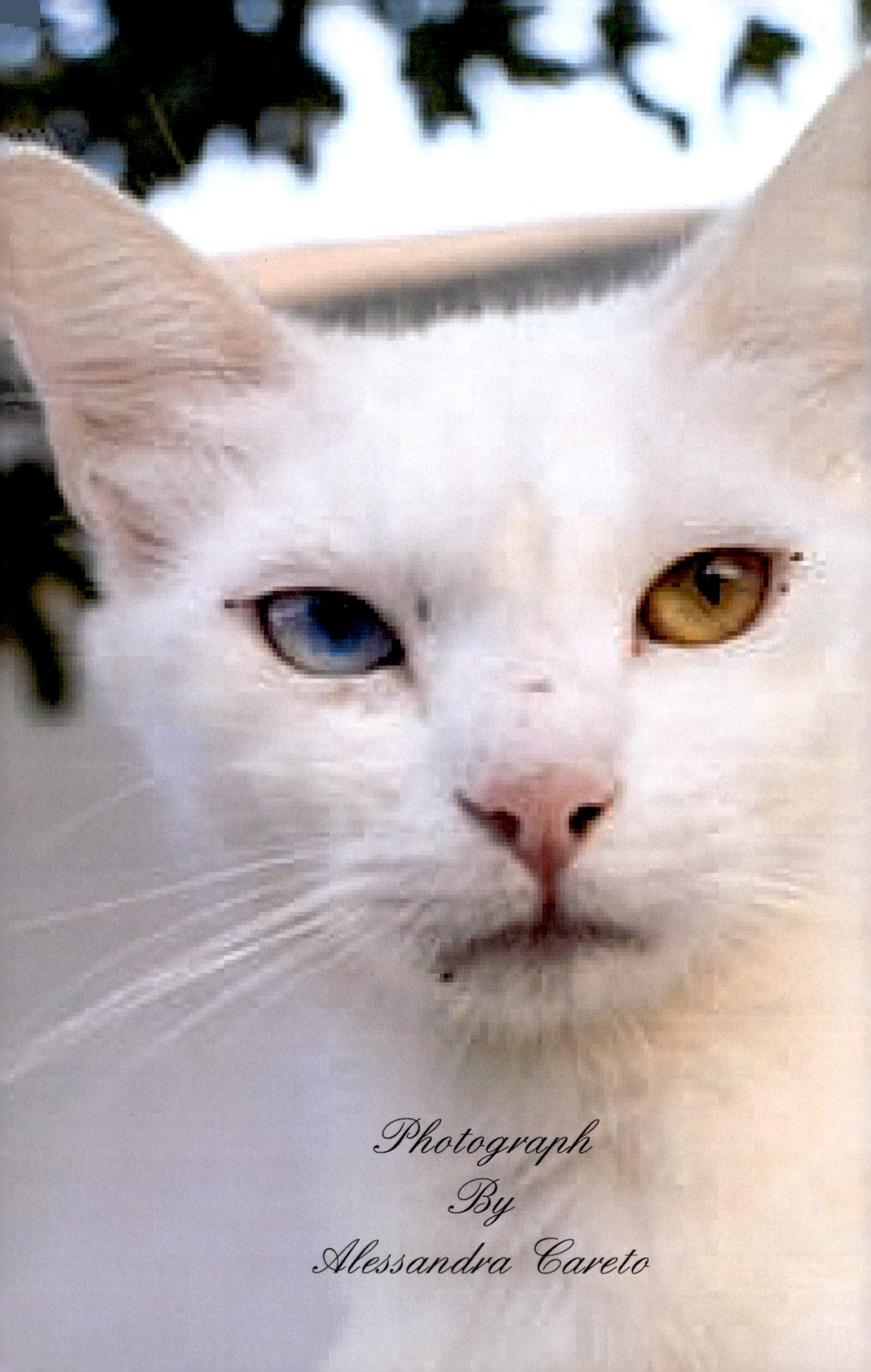

Photograph
By
Alessandra Careto

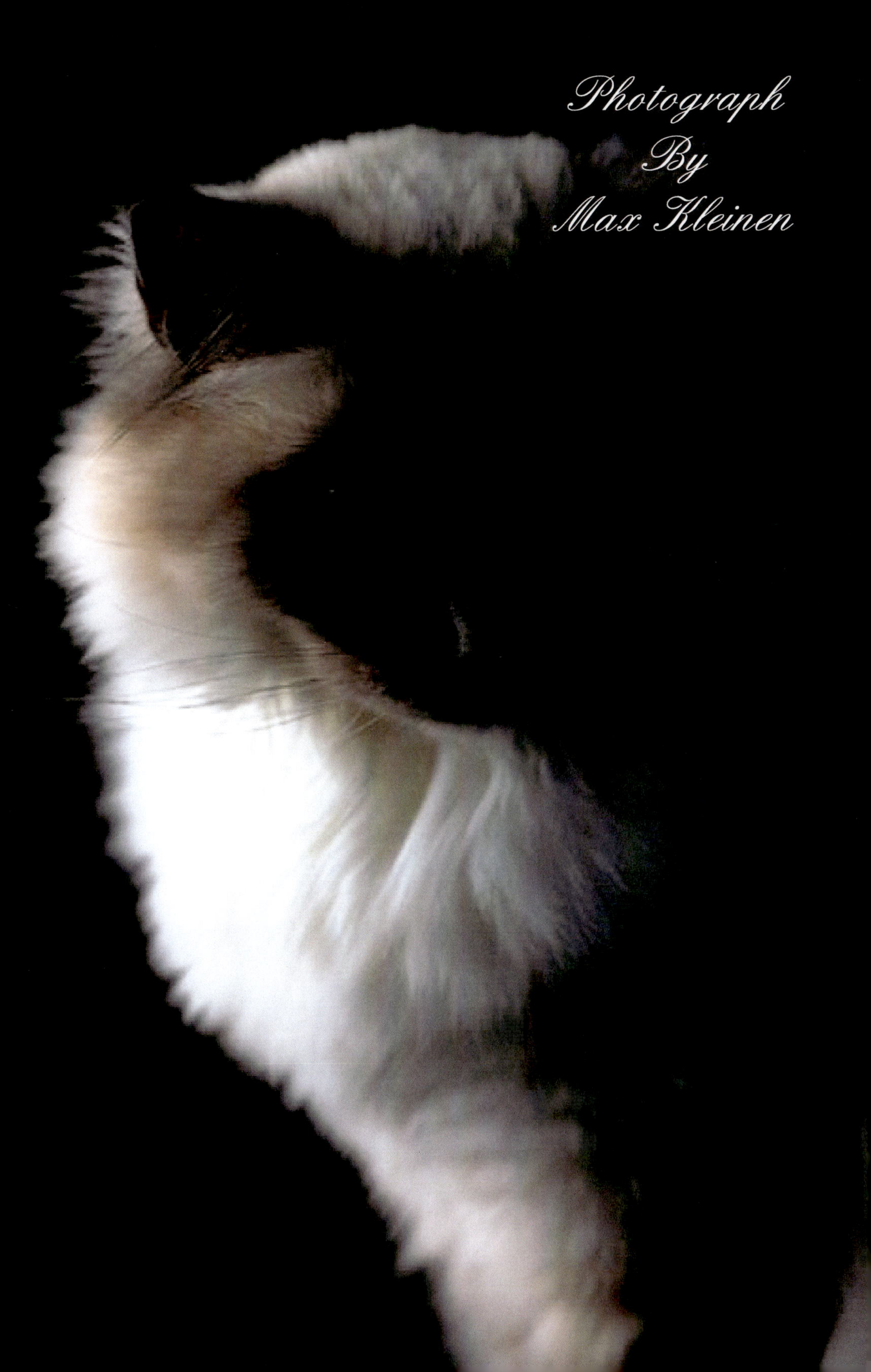
Photograph
By
Max Kleinen

The Lucky Neko Photographer

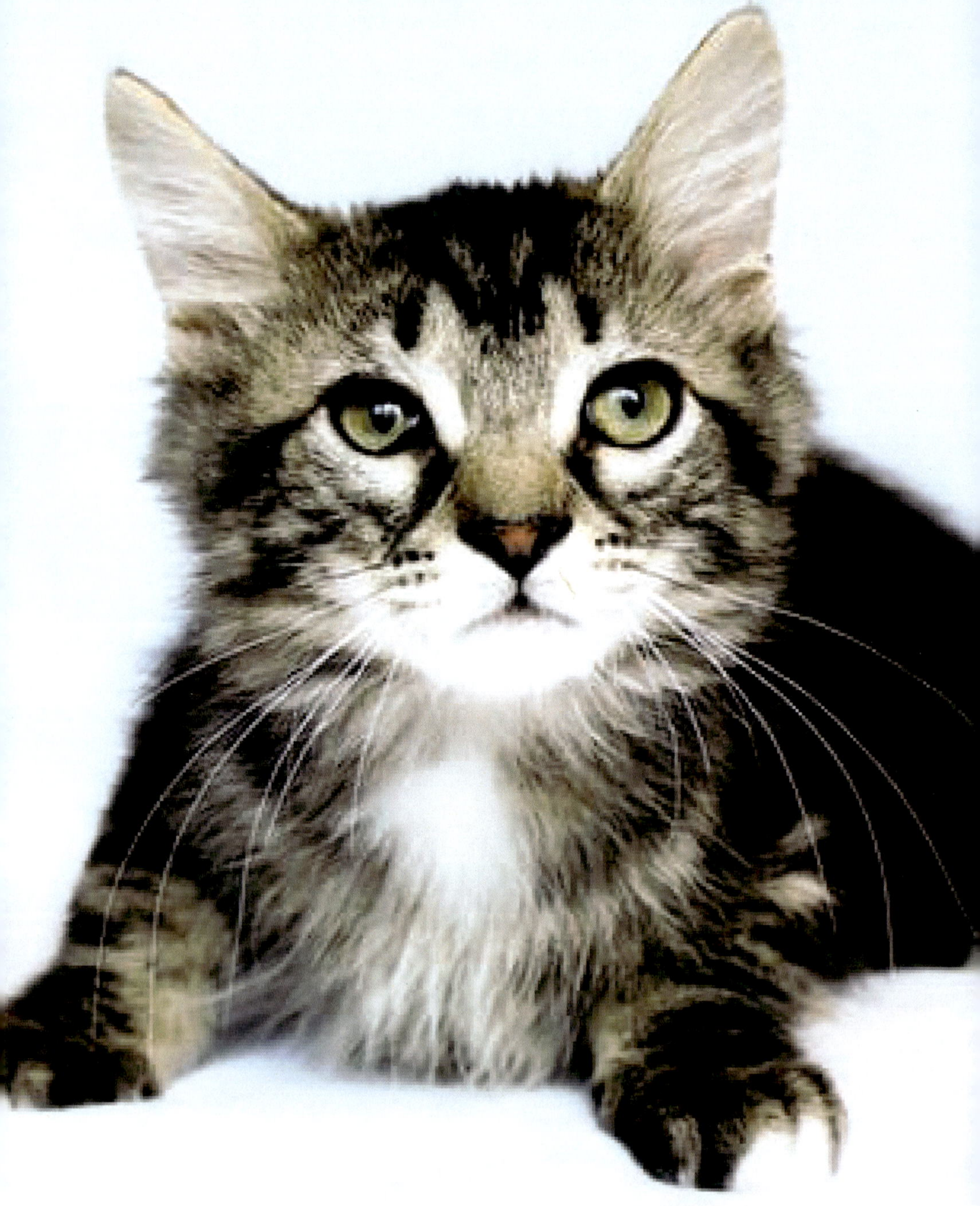

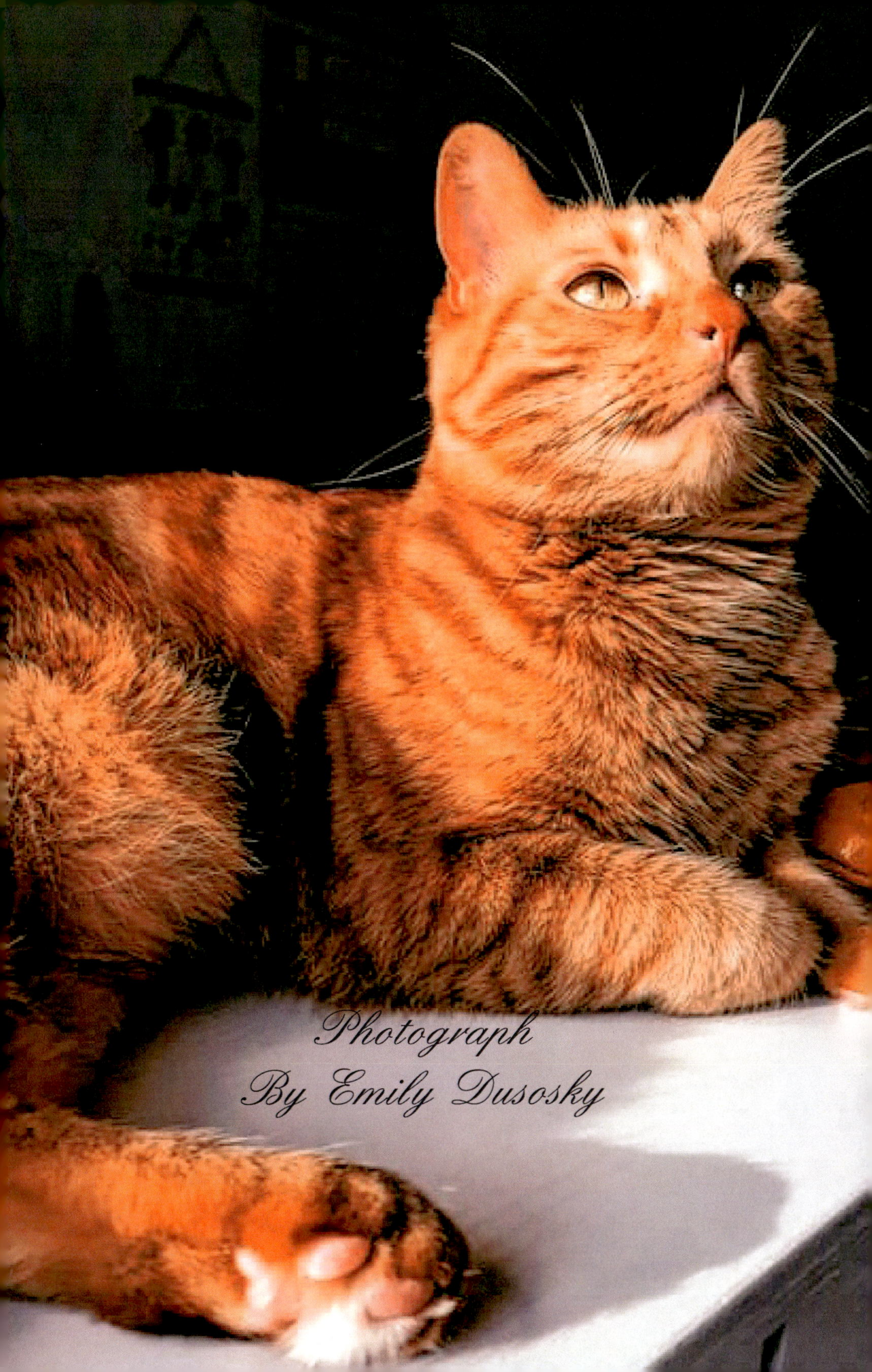

Photograph
By Emily Dusosky

www.ingramcontent.com/pod-product-compliance
Lightning Source LLC
Chambersburg PA
CBRC100808260726
48664CB00028B/1605

9781714579204